MEDEA

M∈D∈A

EURIPIDES · Translated by Oliver Taplin

With an Introduction by Glenn W. Most & Mark Griffith

The University of Chicago Press CHICAGO & LONDON

OLIVER TAPLIN is professor emeritus of classics at the University of Oxford. He is the author of many books, including *Greek Tragedy in Action, Greek Fire, Homeric Soundings,* and, most recently, *Pots and Plays.* He has also collaborated on several contemporary theater productions.

The University of Chicago Press, Chicago 60637
The University of Chicago Press, Ltd., London
© 2013 by The University of Chicago
All rights reserved. Published 2015.
Printed in the United States of America

24 23 22 21 20 19 18 17 16 15   1 2 3 4 5

ISBN-13: 978-0-226-20345-4 (paper)
ISBN-13: 978-0-226-20359-1 (e-book)
DOI: 10.7208/chicago/9780226203591.001.0001

Library of Congress Cataloging-in-Publication Data

Euripides, author.
   [Medea. English]
   Medea / Euripides ; translated by Oliver Taplin ; with an introduction by Glenn W. Most and Mark Griffith
      pages cm
   Translated from the Ancient Greek.
   ISBN-13: 978-0-226-20345-4 (paperback : alkaline paper)
   ISBN-10: 0-226-20345-X (paperback : alkaline paper)
   ISBN-13: 978-0-226-20359-1 (e-book)
   ISBN-10: 0-226-20359-X (e-book)
   I. Taplin, Oliver, translator. II. Most, Glenn W., writer of introduction. III. Griffith, Mark (Classicist), writer of introduction. IV. Title.
      PA3975.M4T37 2014
      882'.01—dc23
                                    2014018743

⊗ This paper meets the requirements of ANSI/NISO Z39.48-1992 (Permanence of Paper).

MEDEA: INTRODUCTION

The Play: Date and Composition

Euripides' *Medea* was produced in 431 BCE as the first of his four plays entered in the annual dramatic competition. The other plays have been lost: *Philoctetes, Dictys,* and the satyr-play *Theristae* (*The Mowers*). Euripides took the third prize. Although *Medea* is one of his earliest securely dated plays to survive, he was probably over fifty years old when he wrote it and had already been competing in the dramatic contests for more than twenty years.

Some ancient scholars report that, according to Aristotle and his student Dicaearchus (fourth century BCE), Euripides revised a play called *Medea* by a certain Neophron (a prolific and successful rival Athenian dramatist) and passed it off as his own; a few even claimed that Euripides' *Medea* was in fact completely the work of Neophron and should be attributed to him. Various ancient commentaries cite passages from Neophron's *Medea* adding up to about twenty-four lines; these do not coincide exactly with Euripides' play, but they are very similar in content. Modern scholars are divided about what to make of all this: some think that Neophron's *Medea* did indeed precede and influence Euripides'; others have maintained instead that Neophron's play came later and that those who thought otherwise in antiquity were mistaken.

The Myth

Medea is a well-known figure from archaic Greek epic and legend. Her name is derived from words meaning "counsel, plan, cleverness." Grand-daughter of Helios (god of the sun), she possesses magic powers with which she can help or harm male heroes. In this regard she is similar to her aunt Circe. In some versions of the myth, Medea is a goddess, in others a human. She plays a crucial role in the popular ancient Greek epic stories that told how the Argonauts, led by Jason, sailed to far-off Colchis on the Black Sea and overcame various challenges and obstacles in order to bring back the Golden Fleece with them to Greece—all aided decisively by Medea, who, out of love for Jason, betrayed her own family (the rulers of Colchis and guardians of the Fleece) and chose to put her sorcery at his service. It was through her powers and advice that Jason succeeded in putting a dragon to sleep and killing it, then harnessed fierce oxen with which he plowed furrows to sow the dragon's teeth, killed the armed men who sprang up from the teeth he had sown, and then managed to escape from Colchis and avenge himself on his enemies.

After Jason and Medea escaped they took up residence in Corinth, where they had children together. But Jason subsequently decided instead to marry the daughter of the king of Corinth (Creon). It is here that the action of Euripides' *Medea* begins: we see how Medea kills this new bride and her father and the children she had had with Jason, and then escapes from Corinth to Athens. Various ancient poets and local historians, some of them writing before Euripides, mentioned the death of Jason and Medea's children at Corinth—the local cult in which they were honored there is well attested—but gave different explanations for just how the children had died: that the Corinthians murdered the boys in a temple of Hera out of hatred for Medea; or that, after Medea had killed Creon and fled to Athens, leaving her children at the temple of Hera, Creon's relatives avenged themselves by killing the children; or that Medea tried to make the children immortal but something went wrong and they died. The idea that Medea deliberately killed her own children may or may not have been a new invention by Euripides (or Neophron).

After the events in Corinth, Medea goes on to Athens, where she marries King Aegeus and (in some versions) tries to kill his son Theseus. Years later she returns to her homeland Colchis, where she becomes queen. According to some versions, she ends up marrying Achilles after their deaths and reigning with him over the souls of the dead.

Euripides seems to have been particularly interested in Medea: before he composed this play he had already dramatized two other episodes from the myths involving her, one about earlier events (*The Daughters of Pelias*) and one about later ones (*Aegeus*). But both of these plays are lost.

Transmission and Reception

Although *Medea* was not particularly successful when it was first produced, it went on to become enormously popular and influential. It belongs to the group of ten plays by Euripides that were most widely diffused during ancient and medieval times. Its popularity among ancient readers is attested by a dozen papyrus fragments dating from the third century BCE to the sixth century CE. So it is perhaps not surprising that modern scholars have detected what seem to be numerous small interpolations in the text, probably due in some cases to expansion by directors or actors—further evidence for the play's continuing vitality on ancient stages.

Euripides' *Medea* exerted considerable influence upon later Greek and Roman versions of the story. Of Roman tragedies, we possess Seneca's *Medea* and know that Ovid wrote a highly regarded *Medea*, now lost. And the influence of Euripides' play is no less evident in such Greek and Roman narrative epics as Apollonius of Rhodes' *Argonautica*, Ovid's *Metamorphoses*, and Valerius Flaccus' *Argonautica*. Most ancient versions of the Medea story emphasize her magic powers and concentrate on her more terrifying aspects. On south Italian vase paintings of the fourth and third centuries BCE, several of them clearly influenced by theatrical productions, Medea is often displayed killing her children or escaping with their bodies on her winged chariot. Pompeian frescoes show her anguished indecision about whether or not to kill the children. Later Roman sarcophagi frequently depict the terrible death of Creon's daughter and Medea's spectacular escape.

In modern times *Medea* has become one of the very best known of all ancient tragedies. The story of the woman who avenges herself upon her unfaithful husband by killing their children has become part of the popular imagination and has played an important role in such fields as politics (Medea's monologue on the troubles of women was cited regularly in meetings of the British suffragettes), psychoanalysis, and law. Besides the frequent productions of Euripides' play on stages throughout the world in all languages, including ancient Greek—probably no other ancient play has been produced anywhere near as often in the twentieth century—the story has also inspired numerous new versions, including Franz Grillparzer's dramatic trilogy *The Golden Fleece* (1819-21), Christa Wolf's novel *Medea.Voices* (1996), Luigi Cherubini's opera *Medea* (1797), Martha Graham's dance drama *Cave of the Heart* (1946, with music by Samuel Barber), and films by Pier Paolo Pasolini (1969) and Lars von Trier (1988). It has also been depicted in important paintings (Eugène Delacroix, 1862; Gustave Moreau, 1865) and sculptures (Auguste Rodin, 1865-70).

MΣDΣΛ

Characters   N U R S E to Medea
Two S O N S of Medea and Jason
T U T O R to the two sons
M E D E A, princess of Colchis, wife of Jason
C R E O N, king of Corinth
J A S O N, son of Aeson, king of Iolcus
A E G E U S, king of Athens
S E R VA N T of Jason as messenger
C H O R U S of Corinthian women

Scene: Corinth, in front of Medea's house.

(Enter Nurse from the house.)

N U R S E

If only the swift *Argo* never had swooped in between
the cobalt Clashing Rocks to reach the Colchians' realm;
if only pines had never been chopped down among the
  woods
of Pelion to put oars in the hands of those heroic men,
who ventured forth to fetch the Golden Fleece for Pelias.   5
Medea, then, my mistress, never would have sailed
for Iolcus' towers, her heart infatuated with desire for Jason;
nor spurred the daughters of old Pelias to kill their father,
never would have settled here in Corinth   10
with her husband and her sons.
She managed though an exile° to delight the people of the
  land

she'd joined, and gave support in every way to Jason—
life's most secure when there is no conflict
to alienate a woman from her man.   15
But now . . . now hatred rules, and loyal love is sick,
since Jason has betrayed my mistress and their sons,
by mounting the royal bridal bed
beside the daughter of Creon, the monarch of this land.
And so my poor Medea is disdained.   20
She cries, "What of his oaths?," recalls
the solemn pledge of his right hand, and prays the gods
to witness what poor recompense she has received.
Lying without food, she gives her body up to pain,
and has been wearing down the nights and days with tears,   25
since she first found she had been wrongly treated by her
    man.
Never lifting up her eyes from staring at the ground,
she listens to her friends' advice no more
than if she were a rock or sea-surf—
except for when she turns her pale white neck,   30
lamenting to herself for her lost father, country, home,
which she betrayed to join the man who now dishonors her.
She's learned from her catastrophe how much
it matters not to lose your homeland.   35
She hates the children, takes no pleasure in the sight of them.°
I fear that she may plan some new mischief;
her temperament is fierce, and she'll not tolerate
mistreatment—I know too well what she is like.
She fills me with alarm,
that she will stab their livers with a sharpened sword,°   40
entering by stealth the palace where the bed is laid,
and kill both monarch and his daughter's new bridegroom,
and so incur some even graver consequence,
for she is fearsome—
and no one who picks a fight with her
will find it easy to descant the victory chant.   45

(Enter the two boys and their Tutor from the side.)

But here the children come, fresh from their exercise,
and unaware of all their mother's sufferings—
young minds are not inclined to cares.

TUTOR

Old servant of my mistress' house,
why are you standing solitary here outside the doors,
bewailing troubles to yourself?   50
How could Medea want to be left without you near?

NURSE

Old man, you who take care of the young sons of Jason:
when affairs break badly for their masters,
this can affect good slaves as well.   55
And my distress reached such a pitch I felt compelled
to come out here and tell the problems that beset
my mistress to the earth and sky.

TUTOR

You mean she's still not stopped her grieving cries?

NURSE

You've no idea! Her pain's not even halfway through.   60

TUTOR

Poor fool—if I may say that of my betters—
how little she knows yet about the latest downward turn.

NURSE

What's that, old man? Don't hold it back from me.

TUTOR

Nothing—I wish I had not said a thing.

NURSE

Do not, I beg you, hide this from your fellow slave.   65
I shall keep quiet about these matters, if I should.

TUTOR

I overheard a person say—pretending not to hear
as I drew near to where the old men sit
and play their checkers, by the sacred spring of Peirene—
I heard him say that Creon, lord of this land, intends   70
to drive these children out from Corinth, with their mother.
I do not know whether this rumor's true—I only hope it's not.

NURSE

Will Jason tolerate such treatment of his sons
even if he has this feud against their mother?   75

TUTOR

Ancient ties become displaced by newer ones;
and he's no friend to this house here.

NURSE

Then we are ruined if we have to add
this new disaster to the one we've not yet drained.

TUTOR

But you at least keep quiet and spread no word of this—   80
it's not the time to let our mistress find this out.

NURSE

Do you hear how your father's turned against you, children?
I won't say "curse him," since he is my master still.
But he has been exposed as false toward his closest kin.

TUTOR

And who has not? Have you found out so late   85
that every person loves himself more than those close to him,
some justly, some for profit's sake?°
And so the father of these boys does not feel love for them,
because of his new bride.

NURSE *(To the children.)*
All will be well; now, children, go inside.

(To the Tutor.)

And you should keep them well secluded   90
from their mother for so long as she remains
in such an agitated state; don't let them near.
I've seen her cast a savage look at them,
as though she's contemplating doing something to them.
I know for sure she won't relent her anger
until she's struck some victim to the ground—
but when she does, may it be enemies, not friends.   95

MEDEA [singing from inside]
  Oh, in pain, in pain,
  I'm so unhappy, I . . .
  oh for me, for me,
  if only I could die.

NURSE [chanting throughout this scene while Medea continues to sing
from inside]
  As I said, dear children, your mother is stirring
  her passion, bestirring her fury.
  Now hurry indoors; don't stray in her sight,   100
  don't even go near, keep well away
  from her violent mood,
  the wild hate of her passionate will.
  Hurry along, quickly inside.   105
  It is all too clear that she's going to ignite
  this cloud of complaint now billowing
  from its beginning to yet hotter resentment.
  What will she do, now that her heart
  has been so envenomed,
  proud to its core, tough to restrain?   110

                    (Exit the two boys and the Tutor into the house.)

MEDEA *(Inside.)*
  The suffering I have endured, endured,
  calling for bitter lament aloud!
  Accursed children of a hated mother,

I wish you were done for along with your father.
To hell with the family, all of the house.

NURSE

Oh no, terrible! Why should your children 115
share in the guilt of the crimes of their father?
Why should you hate them?
I'm utterly stricken with fear for your safety,
poor children. Rulers have dangerous natures:
subjected to little, controlling much, 120
they are not inclined to relent from their passions.
Better to live in the ways of fair-sharing:
the height of ambition for me is to live out my life
without much, but entirely secure.
The word "moderation" sounds first 125
in our speaking, and is easily best in enactment.
Exaggeration can never provide
sound balance for humans.
And if ever a god gets angered against
some household, the payoff's yet greater disaster. 130

(Enter Chorus of Corinthian women.)

CHORUS [*singing throughout this scene, while the Nurse continues to*
chant and Medea sings from inside]
I heard her call, I heard her cry,
Medea's pain, the Colchian.
So she has still not settled calm?
Old woman, tell. I heard her voice
from deep inside her mansion gates. 135
The sufferings of this household cause
me pain—my friendship's blended close.

NURSE

No household exists any more—it's all gone.
He is possessed by his royal embraces; 140
she is eroding her life away

deep in her chamber, my lady,
her spirit encouraged not the slightest
by any suggestion from any well-wisher.

MEDEA *(Inside.)*
May lightning shatter my skull;
life no longer brings gain. 145
May I find shelter in death,
freed from this hated life.

CHORUS
STROPHE
O Zeus, Earth, and shining Sky,
do you hear the wailing cry
of the inauspicious bride? 150
Why crave for that unwanted bed,
poor woman? Death comes with all speed.
Don't pray for dying, no.
If your husband worships so 155
at his newfound marriage-couch,
don't be torn by him so much.
Zeus will be your advocate;
so don't pine away so much,
wasting for your old bedmate.

MEDEA *(Inside.)*
Artemis and mighty Themis, 160
see the pain that I'm enduring,
I who had my cursed husband
tied by strong bonds of his swearing.
May I see him and his consort
and their palace ripped in pieces,
payment for the ways they dared first
to mistreat me with injustice. 165
O my father, O my city,
after killing my own brother,

in disgrace I had to leave you,
lost my fatherland forever.

NURSE

You hear her calling aloud on Themis
and on Zeus, the protector of oaths 170
binding on humans? My mistress will never
relent from her anger with some petty gesture.

CHORUS

ANTISTROPHE

I wish she would meet with us,
and engage us face to face;
I wish she would heed our voice
to see if she might relent 175
from her heavy-hearted rage
and the passion of her heart.
May I never stand apart
from supporting my own friends.
But, you, please return indoors,
fetch her, bring her here outside, 180
tell her we are on her side;
quick, before she does some harm
against those inside her home—
because her intense distress
comes upon her at a pace.

NURSE

I'll do this—although I'm afraid
that I'll never prevail on my mistress— 185
I'll try as a favor.
Yet she glares like a lioness with new cubs
at anyone who comes close and offers her any suggestion.
You'd be right to conclude that the people 190
of olden times were stupid and lacking in wisdom
when they invented poems
to accompany feasts, celebrations, and dinners,

sweet ornamentations of life.
Still no one has found out the way
to abolish our harrowing griefs   195
with poetic powers
or with songs and elaborate strings—
griefs that result in the deaths and terrible mishaps
that overturn households.
Yet that would have offered us profit:
to medicine these troubles with music.
Why bother with loudly voiced singing for nothing,   200
when feasting is garnished with pleasure?
All by itself the rich banquet provides
full satisfaction for people.

CHORUS

I have heard her tearful moans   205
and the piercing words she cries
out against that guilty husband
who betrayed their marriage ties.
She has borne unjust abuse
and she calls out aloud on Themis,
guardian of the oaths of Zeus,
oaths that ferried her to Hellas   210
over ocean's inky dark,
opening a salt-sea exit
through the daunting Black Sea's lock.

(Enter Medea from the house.)

MEDEA [speaking]
Women of Corinth, I have come outside to show
you have no cause to tarnish me with blame.   215
Understand: I'm all too well aware
that many people are perceived as arrogant—
some privately, others in public life—and there are those
who gather a bad name for idleness by lying low.
Do not suppose there's any justice rests

in people's eyes: they hate on sight,
before they get to know a man's real inner core,   220
although he's done no wrong to them.
And therefore foreigners should take especial care
to be in tune with the society they join—
nor would I give approval even to a native man°
who foolishly offends his fellow citizens through selfishness.
But in my case, this new and unforeseeable event   225
has befallen me and crushed my spirit,
so that I've lost delight in life—I long to die, my friends.
I realize the man who was my all in all
has now turned out to be the lowest of the low—my husband.
We women are the most beset by trials   230
of any species that has breath and power of thought.
Firstly, we are obliged to buy a husband
at excessive cost, and then accept him as
the master of our body—that is even worse.
And here's the throw that carries highest stakes: 235
is he a good catch or a bad?
For changing husbands is a blot upon
a woman's good repute; and it's not possible
to say no to the things a husband wants.
A bride, when she arrives to join new ways
and customs, needs to be a prophet to predict
the ways to deal best with her new bedmate—   240
she won't have learned that back at home.
And then . . . then if, when we have spent a deal of trouble
on these things, if then our husband lives with us
bearing the yoke without its being forced,
we have an enviable life.
But if he does not: better death.
But for a man—oh no—if ever he is irked
with those he has at home, he goes elsewhere   245
to get relief and ease his state of mind.
He turns either to some close friend or to someone his age.°
Meanwhile we women are obliged

to keep our eyes on just one person.
They, men, allege that we enjoy a life
secure from danger safe at home,
while they confront the thrusting spears of war.
That's nonsense: I would rather join   250
the battle rank of shields three times
than undergo birth-labor once.
In any case, your story's not at all the same as mine:
you have your city here, your father's house,
delight in life, and company of friends,
while I am citiless, deserted,   255
subjected to humiliation by my husband.
Manhandled from a foreign land like so much pirate loot,
here I have no mother, brother, relative,
no one to offer me a port, a refuge from catastrophe.
So I would like to ask this one small thing of you:
if I can find some means or some device   260
to make my husband pay the penalty to quit me
for the wrongs he's done, stay silent, please
—also the man who's given him his daughter, and the bride
     herself.°
Although a woman is so fearful in all other ways—
no good for battle or the sight of weaponry—
when she's been wrongly treated in the field of sex,   265
there is no other cast of mind more deadly, none.

CHORUS LEADER
I will do this: you're justified inflicting punishment,
Medea, on your husband. I am not surprised you feel such
     pain.

(Creon approaches from the side.)

I see King Creon coming to announce some new decision.   270

CREON
Grim scowling scourge against your husband—
yes, that's you, Medea:

I proclaim that you must leave this land in banishment,
and take your pair of sons along with you.
And no delay allowed.
I am myself the arbiter of this decree,
and I shall not go home before I have made sure   275
I've thrown you out beyond the borders of this land.

MEDEA

Aiai!
Utter, complete catastrophe for me!
My enemies are in full sail,
and I have no accessible haven
to land me from this storm of hell.
But I'll still ask, although I am so poorly treated: say,   280
what reason have you, Creon, for expelling me like this?

CREON

I am afraid of you—no point in mincing words—
I am afraid you'll work incurable mischief
upon my daughter.
And many things combine toward this fear of mine:
you are by nature clever and well versed   285
in evil practices; and you are feeling bruised
because you've been deprived of the embraces of your man.
And I have heard—so people say—you're threatening
some act against the giver in this marriage
and the taker and the given bride.
Therefore I'm going to move before that happens.
Better to be hated by you, woman, now   290
than to be soft, and later groan for it.

MEDEA

O misery . . . not for the first time reputation's
done me harm and damaged my whole life.
A man who knows what he's about should never have
his children taught to be more clever than the norm.   295

They get a name for idleness, and only earn
resentful spite from citizens.
The stupid ones, if you bring new ideas to them,
will view you as not clever but impractical.
And if you are perceived to be superior   300
to those who are supposed to be the subtle ones,
society will brand you as a troublemaker.
I myself have shared this fate:
because I'm clever, I am resented by some people,
and in some eyes I'm idle and in others opposite to that,°
and for others I'm a nuisance.   305
Yet, in any case, I'm not so very clever . . .
But still, you say you are afraid of me . . . for what?
Becoming victim of some outrage?
No, don't be scared of me, Creon.
There is no call for me to do offence against the king.
What injury have you done me?
You gave your daughter to the man your heart proposed.
It is my husband; he's the one I hate: 310
your actions were, I think, quite sensible.
So now I don't begrudge your happy state—
go on, enjoy your wedding, and good luck to you all!
And let me live on in this country here—
since, even though I have been done injustice,
I'll hold my peace, subdued by those who have more power.   315

CREON

Your words are soothing to the ear;
but I still have a horror that inside your head
you're hatching plans for something bad.
I trust you all the less than I did previously.
A woman acting in hot blood
is easier to guard against—it is the same with men—   320
than one who's clever and stays secretive.
No—on your way immediately; don't give me speeches.

It's fixed, decided, and you have no art that can contrive
to let you stay among us here as enemy to me.

MEDEA

No, no, I beg you by your knees,
and by your newly married daughter.

CREON

Why waste your breath? You'll never change my mind.   325

MEDEA

You're going to banish me,
and feel no pang of conscience for my prayers?

CREON

I am. I don't hold you closer than my own family.

MEDEA

My fatherland, how strongly I recall you now . . .

CREON

And mine, after my children, is my closest bond.

MEDEA

Ah, passion is such a deadly ill for humankind!   330

CREON

Well, that depends upon the luck of those involved.

MEDEA

O Zeus, make no mistake about
who is responsible for all these trials.

CREON

Get out, you crazy woman, and so relieve me of my pains.

MEDEA

Your pains? I have enough of those myself.
I don't need more from you.

CREON

I'm going to get my men to march you off by force.   335

MEDEA *(Seizing his hand.)*
No, no, please don't resort to that, I beg of you, Creon.

CREON
It's clear you're set upon an ugly squabble, woman.

MEDEA
I shall submit to banishment:
that's not the thing I'm pleading for.

CREON
Then why maintain this grip? Why not release my hand?

MEDEA
Please just allow me to remain today, one day,   340
and give me time to fix arrangements for
my banishment, and make provisions for my boys,
seeing that their father does not care enough
to organize a thing for his own sons.
Pity them—you're a father after all: it's only natural
that you should feel some kindness for them.   345
I'm not concerned about myself and exile,
but them—I weep that they're subjected to distress.

CREON
My character is not at all tyrannical;
and often I have suffered harm through my softheartedness.
So now—I'm well aware of my mistake—   350
you shall obtain this none the less.
I tell you clear, however: if the sun god's coming light
still looks upon you and your boys
within the borders of this land, it means your death.
This word of mine is irreversible.
For now, if you must stay, then stay for one day more.°   355
You can't do anything I fear.

(Exit Creon to the side, leaving Medea with the Chorus.)

CHORUS [*chanting*]
Unfortunate woman!°
Oh, oh, sunk in your misery,
where, where on earth can you turn?
to what protector, to what home, to what land   360
to save you from your troubles?
Some god has cast you adrift, Medea, amidst
an unchartable tempest of troubles.

MEDEA
Everything has turned out badly—no one could deny.
But don't suppose this is the way the course will run.   365
There are still struggles waiting for the newlyweds,
and for the man who made this match, big troubles still.
Do you suppose I ever would have groveled to him now
except to gain advantage and resource?
I would not have spent words on him, not taken hold of him.   370
But he has plumbed such depths of foolishness
that, when he could have foiled my plans
by driving me away, he's let me stay for this one day—
the day on which I shall make dead meat of my enemies—
all three: the father and his daughter and my husband.   375
I have a wealth of ways to post them to their deaths,
and I'm not sure which one to make the first, good friends.
Should I engulf the bridal home in flames,
or stab their livers through with whetted blade,
employing stealth to infiltrate   380
the chambers where their bed is laid?
But there's this one obstruction: if I get caught
while entering to work my plot, then I'll be put to death,
and hand my enemies the final laugh.
So best to take the straightest route—
my special inborn skill in drugs—   385
and so by potions send them off.
So be it!
But then what next? Suppose they're dead:

what city then will take me in?
What friend will grant asylum and a home that is secure,
providing safety for my person? There is nobody.
And so I'll bide my time a little while,
and if some stronghold that can keep me safe appears,　　　　390
deceit and secrecy will be my means to make this kill.
If that turns out to be impossible, and I'm exposed,
then I shall take a sword, although it means my death,
and slaughter them myself.
I'll push my daring to its violent end.
For, by the mistress I revere above all, fellow worker,　　　　395
Hecate, who has her place in the recesses of my hearth,
not one of them shall rack my heart with pain
and get away with it.
I shall make sure this match of theirs is turned
to bitter anguish; bitter also that man's
marriage arrangements and attempt to exile me.　　　　400
So down to work, Medea,
don't relax one jot of all your expertise
in schemes and in contrivances.
On to the dreadful test; now's the time to try your mettle.
You see what your position is: you must not become
a laughingstock because of Jason's union with this Sisyphean
　　　dynasty.　　　　405
You're from a noble father and descended from the Sun.
You have the expertise. What's more, we are born women.
It may be we're unqualified for deeds of virtue:
yet as the architects of every kind of mischief,
we are supremely skilled.

(Medea stays on stage.)

CHORUS [*singing*]

STROPHE A

Pure rivers are running their currents upstream,　　　　410
order and everything's turned upside down,
the dogmas of men are exposed as mere sham,

oaths by the gods prove no longer firm ground.
The stories of women shall be about-turned,   415
so that my life shall achieve proper glory,
new value is coming for our female kind,
no longer shall slanders pollute our story.   420

ANTISTROPHE A

The poems of long-ago bards shall no more
portray us as fickle, untrustworthy friends—
bias because lord Apollo forbore
to implant his lyrics in feminine minds.   425
Otherwise we could have answered with songs,
back to the masculine sex, that long years
can easily open up tales of men's wrongs,
no less than their narratives all about ours.   430

STROPHE B

You, Medea, sailed off from
your father's house,
with your heart on fire with love;
and cut your course
in between the matching rocks
of Bosphorus' straits;   435
and you've had to treat as home
an alien place,
where you've lost your marriage bed—
no husband there.
Last, you're driven, stripped of rights,
far from this shore.

ANTISTROPHE B

Dead and gone the bonding charm
of oaths men swear;
Shame's deserted Greece and flown   440
into the air.
You, poor woman, cannot claim
a father's roof,

place to move your anchorage,
sheltered from grief.
And another woman rules
over your bed,
a royal princess, who controls
your house instead. 445

(Enter Jason from the side.)

JASON

This is far from the first time that I have observed
a fiery temper is an uncontrollable disaster.
You could have held on to this place,
even this house, by patiently complying with
the plans of your superiors;
instead, all thanks to your demented rant, 450
you're getting thrown out from this land.
Not that I care about myself: you can go on abusing Jason,
calling him the worst of men indefinitely.
But after all the things you've said against the ruling family,
count it as profit that your punishment is only exile.
I've constantly been trying to calm down 455
the enraged ruler; and I wanted you to stay.
But you refuse to curb your stupid tongue,
forever slandering the king.
And so—exile for you.
Yet even after this I've not deserted my own kin:
I've come because I'm looking out for you, 460
woman, to make quite sure that you do not depart in poverty,
together with our boys, nor under any need.
Exile brings many disadvantages along with it—
and even if you feel the deepest hate for me,
I never could reciprocate ill will for you.

MEDEA

You cheating rat! That's my response to you, 465
the lowest phrase that I can find to fit your cowardice.
You come to us, you come to us,

when you have proved yourself our most detested enemy.
to gods, to me, and all the human race.°
This is not merely daring or self-confidence,
to treat your kin despicably,   470
and then to look them in the eye.
It is the worst of all the ills that plague mankind:
sheer deadness to human decency.
Yet you did well to come—since I can speak,
and ease my spirit, by condemning you;
and you will suffer pain through hearing it.
I shall begin our story from the start.   475
I saved your life—and all the Greeks who went aboard
the *Argo* with you are aware of that—
when you were sent to set the yoke
upon the bulls with breath of fire,
and plant the ploughland with a crop of death.   480
Meanwhile the serpent which kept sleepless watch
over the Golden Fleece, with implicating coils,
I killed—and raised for you the torchlight of survival.
By my own choice I was a traitor to my home and father,
and accompanied you to Iolcus under Pelion—
from impulse rather than from careful thought.   485
I killed off Pelias, so that he died most horribly,
at his own daughters' hands—and thus extinguished his
        whole line.
And after all these favors you have had from me,
you stinking rat, you have betrayed me,
and found a new wife for your bed—
this even though we have begotten sons.
If you had been still childless, then it might have been   490
forgivable for you to hanker for this coupling.
The trust that underlies your oaths is lost:
so I'm not sure if you believe the gods of old
no longer wield their power, or else that novel rules
are now established for mankind—

since you must know full well that you   495
have not made good your oaths to me.
Ah, my right hand, the hand that you so often took,
clasping my knees, how foully you have been
exploited by a cheating coward—
and how mistakenly I aimed my hopes!
Now look, I shall consult you as a friend—
though how can I expect to gain some benefit from you?—   500
yet all the same, by being asked, you'll be exposed
as even worse. Where shall I turn now?
Maybe my father's house?—the very house and fatherland
that I betrayed for you, to travel here.
Or to the wretched daughters of King Pelias?
yes, they would give me a warm welcome back,   505
when it was I who killed their father.
For that is how I stand: object of hatred for my kin at home,
I've made the people whom I should have treated well
my enemies—all for your sake.
And as reward you made me, to be sure,
the happy woman in the eyes of many girls in Greece.   510
O yes, in you I have a husband marvelous and true—
since that is why I am to be expelled from here
to wander as a refugee, devoid of friends,
alone with my poor children, all alone.
That is a fine reproach to grace the new-made groom:
his children beggars wandering   515
along with her who saved your life.
O Zeus, you've given us the clear criteria to test
if gold is counterfeit: so why is there no stamp of guarantee
marked on the human body to discriminate which ones
among our men are fakes?

CHORUS LEADER

When those who have been close collide in conflict,   520
their anger is incurable and terrible.

JASON

It seems I'm going to have to prove myself as orator,
and, like a skillful captain, reef my sails
in to the very edge, if I'm to navigate
before your windy and unbridled talk, woman.   525
For my part, since you emphasize so much my debt to you,
it's my belief that it was Cypris
alone of gods and humans steered my voyage clear of harm.
You may well have a subtle mind,
but modesty forbids me to relate just how Desire   530
compelled you with unerring shafts to keep my body safe . . .
but I'll not go into too fine detail there.
The benefits you really did for me were well and good.
Yet in return for my survival you've received
far greater profits than you have contributed—   535
as I'll explain. First you inhabit Greece
instead of some barbarian land;
you've gotten to experience the rule of justice and the law,
without consideration for the threat of force.
The Greeks have all found out about your cleverness;
you're famous for your gifts.   540
If you inhabited the furthest fringes of the world,
then no one would have heard of you.
I would not ask for vaults of gold, or for the gift to sing
yet more melodiously than Orpheus,
unless my fortune brought me also great celebrity.
So much then for my efforts made on your behalf—   545
it was you after all embarked on this debate.
I turn now to your condemnations
of the royal match that I have made.
Concerning this I'll demonstrate that I was clever first,
second restrained, and third I've been
a constant friend to you and to my sons.   550
No, please keep quiet.
When I moved here from Iolcus land, I brought with me

a number of intractable misfortunes.
So what prescription could I have discovered
more fortunate than to win the hand, although an exile,
of the king's daughter, and to marry her?
Not, as gnaws away at you, because I came to hate   555
sleeping with you, besotted by desire for my new bride.
Nor am I set on rivalry to father many children,
since I've no complaint with those I have—they are enough.
My motive is the highest of priorities:
that is for us to live a prosperous life,
and not go short—remembering that every friend   560
will run a mile from those who are impoverished.
I wish to raise my children as befits my noble house,
and father brothers for these sons I've had by you;
to put them on a par, to unify the line,
and so achieve a happy life.
For you . . . what need of children do you have?   565
Whereas for me it cashes in a gain to benefit
my living sons through those as yet unborn.
Not bad, my long-term planning?
You would agree, if you were not so stung by thoughts of sex.
You women go so far as to believe,
as long as your sex life goes well, then everything is fine;   570
but then if some misfortune strikes the realm of bed,
you count what's best and finest as your deepest hate.
I say it should have been a possibility
for mankind to engender children from some other source,
and for the female sex not to exist.
That way there'd be no troubles spoiling human life.   575

CHORUS LEADER
Jason, you've laid out a speech all sparkling
with fine embellishments, and yet in my opinion,
although I may be speaking contrary to yours,
you're doing wrong with this betrayal of your wife.

MEDEA

I'm very different from most of humankind,
since, in my book, the clever yet unjust speech maker   580
should be punished with the heaviest fine.
For, confident that he can dress injustice in fine words,
he is emboldened to stop short of nothing.
Yet he is not so clever as all that—
which goes for you as well.
So don't come all respectable and eloquent with me.
I have one argument to knock you flat: 585
if you were not a filthy coward, you should
have first persuaded me to give approval
for your knotting these new marriage ties—
not tried to keep it secret from your kin.

JASON

Oh yes, I think it very likely you
would have endorsed my case quite happily,
if I'd but mentioned this new match to you—
considering that even now you cannot bear
to drain away the seething rage that fills your heart.   590

MEDEA

It was not that that led you to hold back;
it was because a non-Greek wife would not, you thought,
enhance your status in your later years.

JASON

Let me make clear: my motive for espousing the royal bed
I now possess was not the woman in it—
but, as I've said before, the wish to keep you safe,   595
and to beget royal siblings for my sons, a safeguard for my
    line.

MEDEA

I would not wish to live a prosperous life
that brings me misery;
nor do I want prosperity that eats away my soul.

JASON

I'll tell you how to change your mind, and to be seen   600
as far more sensible: don't ever take good things
to be objectionable; and don't regard yourself
as miserable when in fact you are most fortunate.

MEDEA

Humiliate me, go ahead!
You can, since you have somewhere you can turn,
while I'm deserted and must leave this land.

JASON

That's what you chose.
Don't try to pin the blame on anyone except yourself.   605

MEDEA

What did I do? Did I betray you, then,
by getting into bed with a new wife?

JASON

No, but by calling down unholy curses on the royal house.

MEDEA

I did. I am a curse upon your house as well.

JASON

Well, I'll participate no more in these adjudications.
But if you'd like to draw upon assistance from my means   610
to help the children and yourself in exile, then say the word.
I am prepared to hand out generously,
and to send tokens to my friends elsewhere
to have them treat you well.
If you refuse this, woman, you're a fool.
Give up your angry fit, and you will be far better off.   615

MEDEA

I have no wish to beg for favors from your friends,
and I will not accept a penny, so do not offer anything to us.
Donations from a low-life cheat confer no benefit.

JASON

Well, all the same, I call upon the gods
to witness that I am prepared to furnish all I can   620
to make provision for the boys and you.
Yet in return you spurn these goods,
and willfully you push away your friends.
As a result your hardships will be all the worse.

MEDEA

Just go. So long away from your bedroom,
you must be overcome with yearning
for your freshly bridled bride.
Go on, perform the newlywed. Perhaps—   625
pray god fulfill this word—perhaps this wedding
will turn out to be a bedding that you mourn.°

(Exit Jason to the side. Medea stays on stage.)

CHORUS [*singing*]

STROPHE A

Desire that overwhelms us
with infatuation
does not encourage virtue   630
and good reputation.
If her approach is gentle,
Cypris makes life blissful,
sweetest of gods; but never
target me, great mistress;
don't draw your golden bowstring
in my direction, winging
me an unerring arrow,
tip besmeared with longing.   635

ANTISTROPHE A

May moderation please me—
that's the gods' best favor;
and may dread Cypris never
shake my heart with fervor;

nor bring on angry quarrels
and unending clashes,
by making me inflamed for   640
other men's embraces.
May she employ her judgment
wisely to encourage
concord, by fairly settling
women's beds in marriage.

My fatherland, my home place,   645
may I be never homeless,
have never the relentless
life story of the helpless,
most pitiable of all pains.
Before that may my death-day
dark overcome this life-day.   650
There can be no disaster
that is more destructive
than to be deprived of
your fatherland, your home place.

I see from my own witness,
not secondhand from others: 655
for you there is no city,
no friend who will feel pity,
not now that you have suffered
the worst that can be suffered.
The man who is ungracious,
may death end his disgraces;
who disrespects his dearest,   660
refusing to unfasten
the latch of honest thinking.
I never shall befriend him.

(Enter Aegeus from the side.)

AEGEUS

Medea, happiness to you:
there is no finer prologue known with which to greet a
friend.

MEDEA

May you be happy also, Aegeus, offspring
of wise Pandion. Where have you come from,   665
to be passing through this country here?

AEGEUS

I've journeyed from Apollo's venerable oracle.

MEDEA

And why did you consult the prophet at earth's navel-stone?

AEGEUS

To find out how I might get children as my heirs.

MEDEA

Good heavens, have you reached your age   670
still childless?

AEGEUS

Some dispensation of the gods has left me childless, yes.

MEDEA

And do you have a wife,
or have you never known the bond of wedlock?

AEGEUS

I have a wife who shares my marriage bed.

MEDEA

And what did Phoebus say to you about begetting children?

AEGEUS

Words far too subtle for a man to fathom.   675

MEDEA

Is it permissible for me to hear the oracle?

AEGEUS

It is—it does, indeed, call for a clever mind.

MEDEA

What did it say? Enlighten me if I'm allowed to hear.

AEGEUS

It told me not to tap the wineskin's jutting spout . . .

MEDEA

Before what action, or before you reach what land?   680

AEGEUS

Before I reach my native hearth.

MEDEA

What motive then has made you sail to this land here?

AEGEUS

There is a man called Pittheus—ruler of Troezen.

MEDEA

The son of Pelops; and most reverend, they say.

AEGEUS

I wish to talk with him about the prophecy.   685

MEDEA

That's good: the man is wise,
and has experience of matters such as this.

AEGEUS

Of all my allies he's the one I hold most dear.

MEDEA

Then fare you well.
And may you get all that your heart desires.

AEGEUS

But what is this? Why are your cheeks all streaked with tears?

MEDEA

Aegeus, my husband has turned out the lowest of the low.   690

AEGEUS

What? Tell me clearly all your discontent.

MEDEA

Jason has done me wrong, although I've given him no cause.

AEGEUS

What is it that he's done? Inform me more precisely.

MEDEA

He's made another woman
mistress of his bed instead of me.

AEGEUS

I can't believe he's acted so despicably as that.   695

MEDEA

It's true. I was his dear, but now I'm disregarded.

AEGEUS

So is he seized by new desire, or does he now detest your bed?

MEDEA

Desire—so great he's not stayed loyal to his family.

AEGEUS

To hell with him, then, if he is as rotten as you say.

MEDEA

This strong desire has led to his alliance with a king.   700

AEGEUS

So who has made this match with him? Come, tell me all.

MEDEA

It's Creon, ruler of this land of Corinth.

AEGEUS

I see: then, woman, I can understand just why you feel so
hurt.

MEDEA

It is disaster for me;
and, what is more, I'm being sent in exile.

AEGEUS

Who by? That's yet another blow you tell me of.   705

MEDEA

It's Creon who is driving me to banishment from Corinth.

AEGEUS

And Jason goes along with this?
I disapprove of that as well.

MEDEA

He claims he is against . . . but still he's ready to put up
    with it.
But I implore you by this beard and by your knees—   710
I am your suppliant: take pity on me
in my misfortune, take pity.
Don't watch me turned into a refugee:
grant me asylum in your land and in your house.
And then may your desire for children meet success,
thanks to the gods, and may you end your days content.   715
You may not realize what a find you've found in me:
for I shall end your barrenness,
and I shall make you potent to seed progeny.
Such are the potions that I know.

AEGEUS

There is a host of reasons, woman,
why I am inclined to grant this favor to you.   720
First, piety to the gods; and then for the fertility
that you assure me of—I'm at my wits' end over that.
This, then, is what I offer you:
if you can once arrive safe in my country,
then I'll do my best to act as your protector there,
as would be only right.

And yet I forewarn you, woman, of this much:°   725
I am not willing to convey you from this land;
but if you can all by yourself get to my home,
then you may claim asylum.
I shall not surrender you to anyone.
But you must get yourself away
out of this country by yourself;
I wish to stay above reproach with my allies as well.   730

MEDEA

Yes, I agree. All would be well for me,
if only I could have from you some surety of this.

AEGEUS

Can you distrust me? What is disconcerting you?

MEDEA

I trust you; but the house of Pelias remains my enemy,
and so is Creon. If you are tied by oath,   735
you would not let them take me from your land,
but if you were agreed with only words,
without an oath sworn by the gods,
you might become on friendly terms with them,
and then comply with their demands for extradition.
For I have no power,
while they are rich, and members of a royal house.   740

AEGEUS

The things you say show ample foresight.
So if you think it best, I'll not refuse to do this thing,
since for me it's safer if I demonstrate
to your opponents that I have good reasons,
while for you your interests gain more security.   745
Tell me the gods to be sworn by.

MEDEA

Then swear by Earth and by the Sun,
my father's father, and the whole pantheon together.

AEGEUS

What to do, what not to do? Go on.

MEDEA

That you will never cast me from your land;
and never, if one of my enemies attempts to take me,   750
never, while you live, abandon me of your free will.

AEGEUS

I swear by Earth and by the pure light of Sun
and all the gods: I shall stay true to all you say.

MEDEA

Enough. But if you fail to keep your oath,
what then should be your fate?

AEGEUS

Those things that are inflicted on the impious.   755

MEDEA

Then go, and fare you well. For everything's in place.
And as for me, I'll reach your land as quickly as I can,
once I have carried through my plans,
and gained the things I want.

CHORUS LEADER [chanting]

May Hermes, the patron of travelers,
usher you safely home;   760
and may you achieve those things
which you so strongly desire,
because you appear to us, Aegeus,
as a man of true nobility.

(Exit Aegeus to the side.)

MEDEA

O Zeus and Justice, child of Zeus, and radiance of the Sun—
now, friends, I'll win the victory against my enemies.   765
I have set out upon the road; and now I have good hope

that they shall pay the price in full.
For in the very place I was most laboring,
this man has now appeared as a safe haven for my plans.
I'll fix the mooring cable to my prow from him,   770
once I have reached Athena's citadel.
And now I'll tell you all my plans:
attend my words, although they are not pleasant words to
    hear.
I'll send one of my servants asking Jason
to come and meet me face to face.   775
And when he's here, I'll reassure him with smooth words
and tell him I agree: that he is marrying well
the royal match he has contracted by betraying us°
and that this brings advantages, and is well planned.
And I'll request my children may stay here—   780
not that I wish to leave them in a hostile land
for enemies to foully treat my children°
no, but so that I can kill the princess by deception.
I'll send them carrying presents for her in their hands,
to take them to the bride so as not to have to leave this land:° 785
a finespun dress and plaited wreath of beaten gold.
If she accepts and puts the finery next to her skin,
she will die horribly, and so will anyone
who even comes in contact with the girl—
such are the poisons that I'll smear upon the gifts.
But now I'll leave that part of the story.   790
I grieve for the deed that I must do then:
that I must kill my sons—
there is no one can spirit them away.
And after I have utterly wrecked Jason's house,
I'll depart this land, escaping from the slaughter   795
of my beloved children, once I've steeled myself
to do this most abominable of deeds.
Because, my friends, to be derided
by one's enemies is not to be endured.
So let it be. What profit have I from my life?°

I have no fatherland, no home, no way to turn from my
    misfortunes.
My first mistake was when I deserted my ancestral home,   800
seduced by sweet talk from a man, a Greek—
with a god's help he will pay me dearly.
Nevermore shall he behold his sons from me alive;
nor shall he have a child with his new-wedded bride,   805
since she must die a horrid death by my strong poisons.
No one should think of me as slight and weak,
or as compliant—quite the contrary:
I'm deadly to my enemies, supportive to my friends.
It's people of this sort whose lives are crowned with glory.   810

CHORUS LEADER
    Since you have shared this plan with us,
    and since we'd like to help you, and promote the human law,
    we tell you: do not do this thing.

MEDEA
    There's no alternative.
    It's understandable you talk like this
    when you have not been made to suffer wrong like me.   815

CHORUS LEADER
    But, woman, can you steel yourself to kill your body's fruit?

MEDEA
    Yes, that's the way my husband can be deepest pierced.

CHORUS LEADER
    You would become the wretchedest of women.

MEDEA
    Then let it be. Meanwhile all words are mere excess.

                                            (To a maid.)

You, go and summon Jason here   820
—you are the one I use for all my tasks of closest trust.
And tell him nothing of the things I have decided,

not if you are true to your mistress,
and if you are a woman born.

(Exit maid to the side; Medea stays on stage.)

CHORUS [*singing*]

STROPHE A

Through their forefather Erechtheus,
derived from gods by birth, 825
long have Athenians prospered,
bred from unconquered earth.
There they nourish their spirits
with arts famous and fine,
ever pacing with light steps 830
the luminous air's shine;
and the Muses, as they report,
the Pierian nine,
at one time gathered there to fill
fair Harmony with breath.

ANTISTROPHE A

And legend says that Aphrodite 835
scoops water with her hand
from the pure river Cephisus,
as all about the land
she blows breezes of sweet breath.
And ever plaiting round 840
a rose garland for her hair,
a sweetly scented crown,
she sends the pleasures of Desire
to sit beside wise Thought— 845
who work together to create
the best of every sort.

STROPHE B

This city of pure waters,
this land of friendly guidance,
how could it give asylum

to you, the children-killer?
hold you, impure, inside it?   850
Just think about the stabbing,
think of the actual murder.
Do not—they are your children—
we utterly implore you,
do not kill your own children.   855

ANTISTROPHE B

Where can you find the will-power,°
where find the heart and vigor
to drive this gruesome daring?
Once you see your own darlings,
how can you then stay tearless,   860
as you stare at their slaughter?
No, you'll not have the power to,
not when they fall and beg you,
no, not to drench all gory
your hands, with heart remorseless.   865

(Enter Jason from the side.)

JASON
Well, here I am at your command.
Although you are so ill disposed, you should not be
deprived of this: I shall pay due attention. Woman,
what new is there that you might want from me?

MEDEA
Jason, I ask you to forgive the things I said.
It's only fair for you to tolerate   870
my angry moods, since there has been
much friendship between us in the past.
I came to words within myself, and scolded in these terms:
"Stubborn, why am I raging and resenting
those who show good foresight?
Why pit myself in conflict with the royal powers   875
of the land, and my own husband?

He's only taking the most advantageous course,
by marrying the princess, and producing siblings for my
   sons.
So should I not relent from anger?
—what is wrong with me?—
the gods are taking helpful care of me.
I must confront the truth: that I have children,   880
and that we are exiles, much in need of friends."
And thinking through these things,
I recognized that I have been extremely stupid,
and mistakenly felt outraged.
So now I give approval; I believe you've shown good sense   885
in forging this new kinship tie on our behalf—
it's I have been the fool.
I should have been there sharing in your plans,
advancing them: I should be waiting on your bed,
and gladly taking care of your new bride.
We . . . I do not say we're evil,
but we are just what we are . . . we women.   890
So you should not yourself
behave like us, and bandy trivial disputes.
I'm sorry, I admit I had it wrong back then;
but now I've thought things through more sensibly.
Children, my children, leave the house,
come here outside.

            (The two boys and the Tutor come out from the house.)

Embrace your father, talk to him along with me,   895
and with your mother now be reconciled from enmity
against those who should be near and dear.
We have made peace, and all our anger is dissolved.
Take his right hand.
Ah me! That makes me think of hidden wrongs.   900
Will you live many years, my children,
to reach out your loving arms like this?

Poor fool, how close to tears I am, how racked by fear.
Here am I making up my quarrel with your father at long
    last,
and yet my tender sight's all blurring full of tears.   905

CHORUS LEADER
A glistening tear has brimmed out from my eyes as well.
I hope this present wrong may not advance yet further.

JASON
I like this thinking, and I don't blame those things,
because it's only natural for females to be jealous,
if some alien partner° gets imported to her bed.   910
But now your feelings have been altered for the better,
and you've recognized, eventually, the winning plan.
These are the actions of a woman who is sensible.
For you, my boys, your father has, with careful forethought,
arranged, thanks to the gods, complete security.   915
It's my belief that you, with your new brothers,
shall enjoy the foremost standing in this land of Corinth.
Your simple task is to grow up; the rest your father manages;
and with some favorable god, I hope to see you thrive,
and come to full maturity, superior to my enemies.   920

                                                    (To Medea.)

But you . . . why are your eyes engulfed with glistening tears?
Why turn your pallid cheek away?
Why not be glad to hear these words from me?

MEDEA
It's nothing. I was only thinking of the children . . .   925

JASON
Don't worry. I'll ensure that all goes well for them.

MEDEA
I shall do as you say, and take your good advice.
But woman is a tender creature and inclined to tears.°

JASON

But why on earth such grieving for the children here?

MEDEA

I gave them birth. And when you prayed
for life for them, a pang came over me   930
in fear for whether this would come to be.
But of the things you came to talk with me about:
some we have discussed, and there are others I have yet to
  mention.
Since the ruler has decided he will banish me,
I shall depart this land, an exile—
this is best for me, I know full well, and not to stay   935
and live where I might trouble you and the royal family,
since I'm considered hostile to this house.
But for the boys: if they're to be brought up by you,
you must beg Creon not to make them leave this land.   940

JASON

I'm not so sure I can persuade him, but I have to try.

MEDEA

At least then get your wife to beg her father
not to make the children leave this land in exile.

JASON

A good idea. And I believe I can persuade her—
if she is a woman like the rest of them.   945

MEDEA

I shall myself take part in this attempt as well:
I'll send her gifts, by far the most exquisite
known to humans of our times—
a finespun robe, and plaited wreath of beaten gold.°
And I'll have the children carry them.
One of you servants, bring the finery   950
out here as quickly as you can.

(She sends a maid into the house.)

She'll win good fortune in innumerable ways,
not only one: she'll get in you the best of husbands
as her bedmate, and acquire the finery   955
that Helios, my father's father,
handed down to his descendants.

(The maid enters from the house, bringing out to
Medea gifts which she hands to the two boys.)

Here, boys, take hold of these fine wedding gifts;
go and present them to the blessed royal bride.
She'll have no reason to complain at these.

JASON

You're being foolish: why deplete your own resources?
Do you believe the royal house is short
of dresses—short of gold, do you think?   960
Preserve these things; don't hand them out.
For if my wife holds me of any value, she'll estimate
my wish above material possessions, I am sure of that.

MEDEA

No, not your way. They say that gifts persuade the gods, even;
and gold means more to humans than a million words.   965
She has the divine touch; for now
the gods are raising her; she is the young empress.
And I would trade my life, not merely gold,
to get my boys reprieved from exile.
Now, boys, proceed inside the splendid palace,
and implore your father's newfound wife, my mistress;   970
beg her not to make you leave this land—
and give this finery to her. This is what matters most:
she must receive these gifts with her own hands.
Now quickly, off you go.
May you succeed and bring your mother
good reports about the things she longs to get.   975

(Exit the two boys to the side, with Jason and the Tutor.)

CHORUS [*singing*]

STROPHE A

Now I've no hope for them, no longer,
the children cannot live, no longer;
they are already gone to slaughter.
The bride, unhappy girl, will take it,
the golden diadem, will take it;
and she shall set the crown of Hades   980
around her head—her hand will place it.

ANTISTROPHE A

The charm and the unearthly glitter
will lure her to enfold around her
the robe and gold-entwined tiara.
She's dressing up to hold her wedding   985
down with the dead. Now she is heading
for such a trap, a fate so lethal,
she can't escape from disaster.

STROPHE B

As for you, sad man, you've tied
a fatal knot with kings,   990
not knowing that it brings
the end of your boys' life,
and cruel death for your bride.
You were, unfortunate,
so wrong about your fate.   995

ANTISTROPHE B

And I feel pain with you,
sad mother of the two,
you'll strike your children dead,
all for the marriage bed
your husband has betrayed—   1000
now he holds in your stead
another as his wife.

(*The Tutor and the two boys enter again from the side.*)

TUTOR

Mistress, here are your sons, reprieved from banishment.
Also the princess has received the wedding gifts
delightedly with her own hands.
So all's plain sailing for your boys in that direction.
What's this?
why rooted there confounded when you've done so well?   1005
Why turn your pallid cheek away?°
Why not be glad to hear these words from me?

MEDEA

Ah me!

TUTOR

This tune is not in harmony with my report.

MEDEA

Ah me, again!

TUTOR

Can I be bringing news
of some misfortune I don't know about,
mistaken in believing my report is good?   1010

MEDEA

The news you've given is the news that you have given.
I don't hold that against you.

TUTOR

Then why cast down your eyes and shed these tears?

MEDEA

There's no avoiding it, old man:
the gods and I, with my bad thoughts,
have engineered this outcome.

TUTOR

Take comfort. You shall yet come back,   1015
thanks to your children's influence.

MEDEA

I shall myself fetch others back before that day,
to my own pain.

TUTOR

You're not the only woman to be sundered from her children.
You are a mortal, and must endure misfortunes.

MEDEA

Agreed. But go inside and make provision
for the children's daily needs.   1020

(Exit the Tutor into the house; the two boys stay on stage.)

O children, O my children,
you two have a city and a home,
and you shall leave me in my misery
to live for always there, cut off from your mother.
Meanwhile I'm heading for another country as an exile—
too soon to have enjoyed you, to have seen   1025
you happily grown up, too soon to decorate
your wedding bath, your wife, your marriage bed,
and raise up high the ceremonial torch—
unhappy in my willfulness.
For nothing, children, have I nurtured you,
for nothing gone through labor, and been raked with pain,   1030
enduring the sharp agonies of giving birth.
I used, poor fool, to pin all sorts of hopes on you:
that you would care for me when I was old,
and lay me out with your own hands when I was dead—
that's something people value highly.   1035
But now . . . this lovely kind of thought is finished now.
Deprived of you I shall drag through my bitter, painful days.
And you shall never see your mother more
with those dear eyes of yours, once you're transported
to another kind of life.
Ah, ah
why look at me like that, my little ones?   1040

why smile what is to be your latest smile of all?
Ah, ah,
what shall I do? My passion has all melted, women,
now that I see my children's shining looks.
I cannot, no.
Good-bye to all my former resolutions:
I shall convey my children from this land.   1045
Why should I use what's bad for them
to pierce their father's heart,
and so inflict upon myself double the pain as well?
No, I shall not. So good-bye, my resolutions.
But stop, what's wrong with me?
Do I want to be a laughing-stock,
and let my enemies get off scot-free?   1050
I must endure. It is mere cowardice
to even let such feeble words into my mind.
So, children, go inside.

(The two boys stay on stage.)

Let anyone who thinks it wrong to stay
near to my sacrifice look after matters for themselves;   1055
I'll not unnerve my hand.
No, no, my heart, do not enact these things, I beg of you;°
just let them be, show mercy for the children.
They can live there with us, and bring you gladness.
No, by the avenging demons of the world below,
I swear, there is no way that I shall leave   1060
my boys among my enemies so they
can treat them with atrocity.
Now they are bound to die in any case, and since they must,
it will be me, the one who gave them birth,
who'll be the one to deal them death.
In any case these things are fixed and inescapable.
She has the garland on her head already;   1065
the princess-bride is in her death throes
in the gown, I'm sure of it.

But now, because I am about to tread
the most unhappy of all roads,
and I am sending these two down a track more wretched yet,
I want to say some parting words to them.
Come here, my children, reach out
your arms and hold your mother tight.   1070
O dearest arms, and dearest mouth,
and shapeliness, and children's noble looks!
May you fare well, but over there:
your father has despoiled what there is here.
Your lovely touch, your silken skin,
and such sweet children's breath!   1075
Away, go, go. I can no longer bear to look at you,
I'm overwhelmed by pain.
I realize what evil things I am about to do,
but it's my anger dominates my resolution—anger,
the cause of all the greatest troubles for humanity.   1080

(Exit the two boys into the house; Medea stays on stage.)

CHORUS [*chanting*]
Repeatedly I have explored
ideas of intricacy
and entered on deeper disputes
than usually womankind does.
We have inspiration as well   1085
that prompts dialogue leading truly
to wisdom (not everyone,
you'll only discover a few,
one woman among many more,
with true inspirational thought).

My conclusion is this: 1090
that people who've never had children,
and have no experience of them,
are certainly happier far

than those under parenthood's yoke.
With no opportunity to
experience children as joy,
nor as causes of pain— 1095
they steer clear of many ordeals.

And those with that sweetness of growth,
with children as plants in their house—
I notice how all of the time
they are worn down to shadows with cares. 1100
Struggling with how to nurture good health,
then how they can leave them well off ...
and, after that, it's still unsure
just whether this labor is spent
to raise them as bad or as good.

And lastly I have to include 1105
one final disaster of all
for humans. Supposing all's well—
they've put aside plentiful means,
their children have grown to the full,
their character makeup is good—
still, if destiny has it this way, 1110
then Death takes their bodies below,
abducting your child's lovely life.
Yet how can it profit the gods
to pile upon humans this worst
and most agonizing of blows— 1115
a fine for the bearing of children.

MEDEA

I have been waiting for some time, my friends,
to see how things develop over there.
At last I see this man of Jason's coming;
his labored breathing shows he brings grave news. 1120

(Enter Servant from the side.)

SERVANT

Oh, you have done a terrible, atrocious crime,°
Medea. Run, run fast away—by sea-borne craft
or earth-borne chariot—take what you can.

MEDEA

And what has happened that demands escape like this?

SERVANT

They're dead—your poisons
have just destroyed the princess and her father Creon.   1125

MEDEA

That's excellent news—
I'll always number you among my friends and benefactors.

SERVANT

What's that? Can you be sane? Or are you mad?
To devastate the royal house, and then be pleased,   1130
and not afraid to hear of things like this?

MEDEA

I too have things I could reply.
But take your time, my friend, and tell me all:
how did they die? You'll give me twice
the pleasure if they met their end most horribly.   1135

SERVANT

When your two children and their father had arrived
inside the palace of the bride, we servants
who were anxious for your troubles were well pleased—
a lively rumor had just reached our ears
that you and your spouse had laid your former strife to rest.   1140
One of us kissed your children's hands, another kissed
their shining hair, and I myself accompanied
the youngsters to the women's chambers with a joyful heart.
The mistress we now wait upon instead of you,
before she saw your pair of boys,   1145
was glancing with excited looks toward Jason.

But then she covered up her eyes and turned away
her pallid cheek to show how much she loathed
the children's access there.
Your husband then set out to mollify
the woman's angry mood by saying this: 1150
"You should not be unfriendly to your own;
give up this anger and turn back your face.
Consider as your own, your dear ones, those your husband
    does.
Why not accept these presents, and entreat
your father to release the children from their banishment?—   1155
please, for my sake."
Once she had looked close at the finery, she was unable to
    resist;
she went along with everything her husband wanted.
And before he and your boys had gone
far from the palace, she unwrapped
the ornamented gown, and draped it round herself;
and placed the golden wreath about her curls;   1160
holding a burnished mirror to arrange her hair,
she smiled to see the lifeless image of her body there.
Then rising from her throne, she moved around the room,
stepping lightly on her snow-white feet.
She was enraptured by the gifts, and kept on looking down   1165
to check the dress was straight against her ankle.
But then there came a horrifying sight to see:
her color altered, and, with limbs convulsing,
she lunged sideways, collapsing on her throne,
and only just avoided falling on the floor.   1170
And some old serving woman, thinking that the fit
must be inspired by Pan, or through some god,
raised up the ritual glory cry—
until, that is, she saw white flecks of foam
discharging from her mouth,
her eyes contorting in their sockets,
her skin all drained of blood.   1175

Then she let out a piercing scream,
in answering discord to her earlier cry.
Immediately one maid set off toward
her father's chambers, and another to report
the bride's collapse to her new husband.
The building echoed through with hectic footsteps.   1180
After about the time that it would take a sprinting runner
to arrive at the finish of a two-hundred-meter racing track,
the wretched girl awakened from her silenced voice
and tight-shut eyes, and moaned a dreadful cry of pain.
Two pincer torments were invading her: 1185
first the golden band around her head spat
an astounding fountain of incendiary fire;
and then the clinging fabric, given by your boys,
began to eat into the poor girl's milky flesh.
Engulfed in flames she rose up from her throne,   1190
and bolted, shaking hair and head this way and that,
attempting to throw off the wreath.
But still the gold clung tightly by its fastenings;
and when she shook her hair,
instead the blazing doubled in intensity.
Then, overcome by agony,
she crumpled to the ground, unrecognizable   1195
to anyone except her parents' view.
The position of her eyes was not distinct,
nor any feature of her pretty face;
and blood was trickling from her crown, mixed sputtering
    with fire.
Her flesh was dripping from her bones like tears of resin, 1200
melted by the hidden action of your poison's jaws.
It was a fearsome sight, and all of us
were scared to touch her corpse—
forewarned by what had happened.
Her father, ignorant, poor man, of the disaster,
ran into the room and came upon her body.   1205
He cried aloud and flung his arms about her,

kissing her, and said: "O my poor child,
which of the gods has cut you down
so undeservedly like this? Which has bereaved me
of your life, an old man at death's door?
If only I could die with you, my child."   1210
When he had finished his lament,
and tried to stand his aged body back upright,
he found that, as with ivy gripping laurel branches,
he was held tightly by the finespun robe.
The struggle then was terrible.
While he did all he could to straighten up his limbs,   1215
she tugged him down again.
And if he tried to pull by force,
she wrenched the old man's flesh from off his bones.
And in the end he was exhausted and gave up the ghost,
poor man, no longer strong enough to fight the dreadful end.
And so they lie there corpses, daughter and old father, dead,°   1220
beside each other, a disaster that cries out for tears.
For me, your fate must lie beyond my scope;
you will discover for yourself
the payback of your punishment.
But as for human life, I think of it—
not for the first time—as a flitting shade.
I'm not afraid to say that those who seem to be so clever   1225
and who take such trouble over making speeches, those are
the very people who are guilty of the worst stupidity.
No human is a truly happy man:
it might be some are luckier than others
when prosperity flows with the tide . . .   1230
but truly happy—no.

                                          (*Exit Servant to the side.*)

CHORUS LEADER
    It would appear that on this day the god
    is rightly loading many evils onto Jason's back.
    O wretched daughter born of Creon, how much we pity you°

for your misfortunes. You've had to go away
to Hades' house, thanks to your union with Jason.   1235

MEDEA

My deed has been decided, friends—
as quickly as I can I'll end the children's lives,
and move on from this land.
I must make no delay, and give no time
for someone else's crueler hand to slaughter them.
Now they are bound to die in any case;   1240
and since they must, it will be me, who gave them birth,
who'll be the one to deal them death.
Come, come, my heart, it's time to put your armor on.
What use postponing now the evil deed,
inevitable acts that must be done?
Advance, my wretched hand, and grip the sword,
grip hard, and make toward life's painful finish line.   1245
No cowardice, and no remembering your children,
how they were your dears, or how you gave them birth.
Instead for this one fleeting day forget that they are yours,
and afterward take time to grieve.
Although it's you who's killing them,
they were your lovely babes.
And I'm a woman made of sorrow.   1250

(*Exit Medea into the house.*)

CHORUS [*singing*]

STROPHE A

I call on Earth and you, Sun, full
illumination,
look down and see this woman's foul
abomination,
before she strikes her deadly blow,
infanticidal.
Since they're descended from your glow,   1255
celestial, golden—

a fearsome thing for divine blood
in desecration
to fall to earth by human deed.
Fire transcendental,
great god of light, restrain, detain
her, exorcising
out from the house this deadly bane,
avenging demon.   1260

ANTISTROPHE A

In vain your toil for children, void,
evaporated;
in vain you bore the pair you loved,
obliterated,
you who escaped those narrow crags,
the most forbidding,
between the cobalt Clashing Rocks,
the never yielding.
Why does such heavy anger load   1265
you, soul-destroying?
Why does blood demand more blood?
For internecine
kin-murder brings for us humans
extreme pollution;
kin-killers bring down on their homes   1270
concordant anguish.

ONE BOY   (Inside.)
No! help, help!

CHORUS [singing]

STROPHE B

You hear the children? You hear their shout?°
O wretched woman, your cursed fate!

ONE BOY
What can I do to get free from my mother's grip?

THE OTHER BOY   *(Inside.)*
I see no way, dear brother—we are lost.

CHORUS [*singing*]
So should I enter? Yes, I choose   1275
to fend off murder from these poor boys.

ONE BOY   *(Inside.)*
Yes, for god's sake, help—now is our hour of need.

THE OTHER BOY   *(Inside.)*
The net, the sword are closing in on us.

CHORUS [*singing*]
So you are really made out of iron,   1280
or out of granite. You will cut down
the lives you nurtured from your womb's field,
doom them to slaughter at your own hand.

ANTISTROPHE B
I've heard of only one woman past,
who killed the nurslings of her own nest.
And that was Ino, sent mad by the gods,
when Hera drove her wandering away from home.   1285
She leapt down into the salty waves,
wickedly drowning her clutch of babes.
She pressed her steps from land into the sea,
and died herself, along with her two sons.
Can there be any event so foul   1290
that it remains still impossible?
The bed of women, love-bed of night—
how many troubles are caused by your might.

(Enter Jason from the side, alone and sword in hand.)

JASON
You women standing by this building here,
is the perpetrator of these dreadful things inside—Medea—

or has she run away in flight?   1295
She's going to have to hide herself deep underground,
or lift herself on wings high in the air above,
if she is to avoid due punishment from this royal dynasty.
Or does she think that she can kill the rulers,
and escape from this house here scot-free?   1300
But it's not her I came about:
much more my children.
Those that she has done damage to will do the same to her:
I've come to save the lives of my two sons,
and stop the kinsmen from inflicting harm
on them in retribution for the awful murder
that their mother has committed.   1305

CHORUS LEADER
O Jason, you unhappy man, you've no idea
how far you are advanced in troubles,
or you never would have said those words you did.

JASON
What's this? I don't suppose she wants to murder me as well?

CHORUS LEADER
Your boys are dead, dead by their mother's hand.

JASON
What are you saying, women? You have shattered me.   1310

CHORUS LEADER
Your children live no more—of that be sure.

JASON
Where did she kill them? Indoors, or outside the house?

CHORUS LEADER
Open the doors, and you will see your murdered sons.

(Jason tries to force open the doors.)

JASON

Quickly, undo the bars; quick, servants,
release the bolts, so I may see this double havoc   1315
both those who are dead, and her—so I may punish her.°

(Medea appears above, in a flying chariot,
with the bodies of their two sons.)

MEDEA

Why rattle at these doors, and try to force them open?
Searching for the bodies
and for me the one who did it?
Then abandon all this effort.
And if you have some need of me,
then speak up if you wish.   1320
But you shall never lay your hands on me—
you see what kind of vehicle the Sun,
my father's father, has bestowed upon me,
as protection from unfriendly hands.

JASON

You thing of hate, woman most loathsome
to the gods, and me, and all humanity.
You who could steel yourself to drive your sword   1325
into the children you yourself had borne;
and you have ruined me with childlessness.
Now you have done these things,
how can you dare to look upon the sun and earth,
when you've committed this abominable act?
To hell with you. Now I see straight: back then I was not
    thinking,
when I conveyed you from your home   1330
in a barbarian land to my household in Greece—
already then a powerful evil,
traitor to your father and the country that had nurtured you.
The gods have sprung on me the demon of revenge
that came with you, because you killed

your brother at the hearth, and then embarked
upon the *Argo*'s glorious deck.   1335
You started out from things like that;
and then, when you had married me
and borne my children, you murdered them—
all for the sake of sexual pride, the bed.
No woman born a Greek would ever have gone through
with such a crime; yet I saw fit to marry you,   1340
in preference to one of them—a loathsome
and destructive union it has proved to be for me.
A lioness not woman, you,
more cruel in nature than the Etruscan Scylla.
But not even with a thousand insults
could I pierce your skin, so toughened is your callousness;   1345
so go to hell, foul creature, and defiled with children's blood.
All I can do is grieve for my own destiny.
I never shall enjoy my new-laid marriage bed;
I never shall share words again
with these two children that I sowed and bred,
not in this life—no, they are lost to me.   1350

MEDEA
I might have contradicted you at length,
if it were not that father Zeus knows well
how you have fared by me,
and how you have behaved to me.
You can't have thought that you could spurn my marriage bed
and then proceed to live a life of pleasure,   1355
reveling in mockery of me?—
nor could the princess, nor could Creon who set up
this match, and wanted to eject me from this land,
and thought to get away with it.
So go ahead, and call me lioness
and Scylla, occupant of the Etruscan cave.°
I do not mind, since now I've fairly clawed into your heart.   1360

JASON

Yet you yourself must also suffer grief,
and be joint sharer in the sorrow.

MEDEA

Yes, surely, but the anguish is well worth it,
as long as you can't mock at me.

JASON

O my poor children, what a vicious mother
yours has proved to be.

MEDEA

O my poor boys, what a sad end you've met,
thanks to your father's failing.

JASON

It was not by my hand they died.   1365

MEDEA

It was, though, because of your own arrogance
and your new-saddled marriage.

JASON

And you believe it justified
to kill them for the sake of sex?

MEDEA

Do you suppose such troubles to be trivial for a woman?

JASON

It is for one who's sensible:
but everything is bad for you.

MEDEA

These children live no more, and that will pierce you
    through.   1370

JASON

They are still here to bring down vengeance
on your guilt-stained head.

MEDEA

The gods know which one started this catastrophe.

JASON

For sure they know your mind and its full loathsomeness.

MEDEA

Yes, hate away.
The very timbre of your voice fills me with loathing.

JASON

And so does yours with me.
Our terms of parting will be easy.   1375

MEDEA

Then tell me—what am I to do?
I too am keen to bring this to an end.

JASON

Just let me bury and lament for these poor corpses.

MEDEA

Never—because I'll bury them with these my hands.
I'll take them to the shrine of Hera on the Peak
to make sure no one of my enemies   1380
can triumph over them by ripping up their graves.
I shall impose upon this land of Sisyphus
a solemn cult and festival for all of future time,
atonement for this heinous murder.
Then I shall make my way to Athens, country of Erechtheus,
where I shall cohabit with King Aegeus, son of Pandion.   1385
And you . . . you shall, appropriately enough,
meet a rotten end,
cracked on the head by a disintegrating piece
from off the *Argo*'s hulk,
and see the bitter outcome of your union with me.°

JASON [*chanting henceforth*]
*I pray that the children's Avenging Spirit
and Justice for murder may hound you to death.*   1390

MEDEA [*chanting henceforth*]

What god or spirit is going to hear you,
who perjured your oaths, and deceived your hosts?

JASON

Child-killer, pollution!

MEDEA

Back to your home and bury your wife.

JASON

I go, bereft of both my sons.   1395

MEDEA

It's early to lament: wait for your old age.

JASON

My children, my darlings . . .

MEDEA

Not your darlings—but their mother's!

JASON

And that is why you murdered them?

MEDEA

For you, to torture you with pain.

JASON

I ache to enfold my sons,
to touch their dearest lips!   1400

MEDEA

Now you address them with love,
now you desire to embrace,
but then you pushed them away.

JASON

Just allow me a touch
of the delicate skin of my sons.

MEDEA

Unthinkable. Your words are wasted in air.

(Medea flies away in the chariot with the bodies of their sons.)

JASON

Pay attention to this, great Zeus: 1405
how I am driven away;
what I have suffered at the hands
of this polluted, this children-devouring she-lion.
With my every morsel of strength
I cry in my grief, and I call on the gods
to be witnesses,   1410
how you prevent me from touching
the children you killed,
deny me the burial rites for their bodies.
Would that I'd never begotten them,
only to see them lie butchered by you.

CHORUS [chanting]

Zeus stores many things on Olympus;°   1415
gods do many things that surprise us.
The endings expected do not come to pass:
those unexpected—the god finds a way.
That sort of story has happened today.

(Exit all.)

TEXTUAL NOTES

(Line numbers in some cases are only approximate.)

MEDEA

12: Text uncertain.

36: This line is rejected by some scholars as an interpolation.

40-43: Some or all of these lines are rejected by most scholars as interpolations.

87: This line is probably an interpolation.

223-24: These lines are rejected by some scholars as an interpolation.

246: This line is rejected by many scholars as an interpolation.

262: Rejected by many scholars as an interpolation.

304: This line is probably an interpolation.

355-56: Some scholars reject these lines as an interpolation.

357: This line is placed by some scholars after the following one and is rejected by other scholars as an interpolation.

468: This line is probably an interpolation.

626: Text uncertain.

725-29: The order of these lines is uncertain, and some or all of them are rejected by many scholars as an interpolation.

778-79: The first of these two lines, or both of them, are rejected by some scholars as an interpolation.

782: This line is probably an interpolation.

785: Probably an interpolation.

798–99: These lines are rejected by many scholars as an interpolation.

856–57: Text uncertain.

910: Text uncertain.

928: This line is rejected by some scholars as an interpolation.

949: Probably an interpolation.

1006–7: These lines are probably an interpolation.

1056–80: Some or all of these lines are rejected by some scholars as an interpolation.

1121: Rejected by most scholars as an interpolation.

1220–21: Some scholars reject the second of these two lines, or both of them, as an interpolation; in addition, the text of the second one is uncertain.

1233–35: These lines are rejected by most scholars as an interpolation.

1273–74: The order and location of these lines are uncertain.

1316: Rejected by some scholars as an interpolation.

1359: Rejected by some scholars as an interpolation.

1388: Rejected by some scholars as an interpolation.

1415–19: These lines are rejected by most scholars as an interpolation.